"You road I enter upon and look around, I believe you are not all that is here, I believe that much unseen is also here."

– Walt Whitman, from "Song of the Open Road"

"Go…? I don't really go anywhere. You can't move. Anywhere you go, you always there. I'm the universe. How can you move the universe? I mean where am I gonna go? You're here. If you move back to LA and sit down you're still here. Anywhere you go you're always there, man."

– Charles Manson

Acknowledgements

The poems "Στενάχωρο", "X" and "On a Winter Morning included in this collection have previously appeared in Snow Lit Rev, Issue 5, Fall 2017.

CONTENTS:

Standing on the Sun I	1
Going	2
The Space Between	6
The Vagabond Poet with the White Dog	8
Standing on the Sun II	12
X	14
Carte de Tendre	16
Colonized	18
Standing on the Sun III	23
Στενάχωρο	25
Bimarian	26
Native Stranger	28
Standing on the Sun IV	30
On a Winter Morning	33
Time over Place over You over Me	34
Gathering Crumbs	36
Standing on the Sun V	39

Standing on the Sun

i

Ash on your palms
and the mandarin scent that lingers in the
grooves of skin that you lick
to see the future
you can't recall. Your language will take you some-
where you will know what comes next
before you take the step. One monkey
won't stop the show — the
train keeps rolling through. The steel will squeeze on by
through the air you can't abide, thick and
sharp like curdled milk and
diamond sheets. And your boxcars of
words and shrugs and furrowed
brows and hugs will carry on to mean
the world in a spongy madeleine,
until it stops, halting
jolt, sparks and the works —
you don't know the drill
but you will,
but you will.

Going

                                                  somewhere
      far
from here
                                                   somewhere
             far from
             l I n g u I s t I c m a z e s
                                     somewhere far from
   familiar this and   that somewhere far
   from this   and this   some
where some thing some time some place
             where everything is
             malleable
                               somewhere   un
        built on a tabula
          rasa   white pentelikon marble
before Perikles'
      visionary hands
                          still
                                  everycolourwhite
                still   rough, amorphous, veined
         still   somewhere with no
memory
                      and no
expectation
          things happen

       and happen and

           happen somewhere

time   time

   moves and the mind and the cells with it too

           move

         somewhere where trees

  breathe   and the ocean   breathes

and the desert   breathes and the   clouds

  breathe

  and the rattlesnake, the hare,

the nightingale, the deer,

   the eagle, the seal,

     the clam

     all

   breathe and breathe and

breathe   because there is

         nothing

else to do but breathe and breathe   and

     breathe like the ocean like the rustling pine
     needles like the grains
     of sand and the polymorphic   wind

       against the boulders

    caressing and flogging and

| hypnotizing against   the passage
of wave and gust and print and sound   atom
         against atom in this   o
                              m
                  e
                         l   e
                  t   t
                              e

of immaterial
         souls in beautiful
straightjackets –

The Space Between

The map on my wall gets people
asking,
where are the pins? The pins on the
places
you want to see, but don't want to see through eyes
alone
places to soak in the colours, inhale the
sounds,
listen to the stories that float like bubbles above the
smells
of the waterfalls of people in the subway; the
windows
and doors that you wrestle with, the
smog
of the wet grass and dry dirt and damp
sidewalks
ripe with the after-rain fumes of
dog-shit.
Where are the pins? I tell them it is not a scratch
map
where you pin your conquests. And it is not a
scratch

map where you pin your dreams –
stabbed
rigid to the wall. There are not enough
pins
and if there were, there is not enough
space,
and if there was, there is not enough
me.
So the map remains empty on the
wall
on the other side of the infinite space
between
the map on the wall

                                          and my chair.

The Vagabond Poet
with the White Dog

From the Midwest to the Bay
plains and spread out shoe boxes
too many stops to count along the way
to needle strewn sidewalks

Memory doesn't always serve
the precise contours of a history or
is a rosary still a rosary if
the beads have lost their thread

Loyalty is a big white dog
by the name of Sophia or Fiona
asks no questions you don't want
to answer demands

less than a baby mama in Idaho
or Chicago you say you'll go back to
She is the one you say but
it's complicated you see and

Is it coincidence you ask
that strip clubs and writers
seem to go hand in hand in
some cities meccas for the two

you seem to think not
as I pet your white dog who is sat
right on top of the Jack Kerouac plaque
You fan out your collections

like a magician with a deck
of stapled pamphlets yellowed
public library sheets a peddler
of words you announce the themes

ART, LOVE, PSYCHEDELICS, TRAVELS and
DARK MENTAL STUFF I pick
two and we exchange paper
for paper and the loaned ear

and platitudes of this casual
stranger a respite from the silence or
belligerence of the road
you say you will be hitting again

One more thing you say
what would you like inscribed
on your tombstone I'm collecting
what people want to be

remembered by
nothing witty or profound
I flip the question but memory
doesn't always serve

rosaries lose some beads
even on a thread the crackle
meets the filter hourglass
of alley-way encounters some say

reality is stranger than fiction
but in the temporal tumble
drier legend loses its dye
though not always its charm

perhaps it's just as
banal a reproduction
tropes echoed on Columbus
street off bricks that have heard

it all better and before
the cliché of rolling hills, nostalgic
bars, cable cars and vagabond poets
the romance of the Road capital R

a smooth façade to mask the diseased
heart alluring voyeurism illusory
wishfully anachronistic
afternoon in Paris of the West.

Standing on the Sun

ii

Not a bottleneck,
not a tunnel, not a crew
change yard. The bull won't find you, the train
won't sneeze, you won't sleep
on yesterday's news because the train will
no longer be. To make yourself feel
better you will write
home and say you took the polar express,
or something like it, sans
Tom and Santa,
and now it has taken you
through -- That is why you are not
here, because you are
here. The definition is the
compass, your rising north
star, but you cannot sketch over
the sketches already made. So many lines
and zigzags and curliques, you lost
your eraser along the way, somewhere
on the rail tracks and now you cannot
return to retrieve to relive
to relieve. You cannot return,
you cannot return.
The sun holds the direction

at its fingertips as you
stand on its belly button. The rays
are skyrocketing and you don't know
which one to latch onto
as they slice through hollow
space in a straight
line. You were never one
for straight lines.

X

Awareness of absence designated in the site of
absence indicates presence –
indicates. Can intent be expressed if intent is not
to express? Can I dance you my thoughts, my feelings,
my words? How do I tell you what I do, what I do
not, when it is the empty
space, the unobserved, I wish
        to convey – the distance
between. The longing that cannot   echo.
What makes your blue shirt blue?

My thoughts are a footnote upon a footnote on supple concrete,
an x

        upon an x on a map with no
coordinates   tainting it
        with words for things that aren't
words. If   I dance I
        dance with paint on my soles.

It is blue because it is everything but
blue. The light reflects, and you see the one
frequency that isn't
there. Somebody explained the science to me once, but it was in
too many words I didn't   understand.

I still dance.

My invisible
ineradicable
stain.

Carte de Tendre

       You don't know what love is,
you sang to me, our legs pretzeled at the end
of the bed, so I did my research and decided
           to make myself
      a map — maybe, this way,
      I would know.

I sat down with a ruler and pencil and measured out:
      the sea of desire, the volcanoes
of passion, the highways of
      egos, the intersections
of compromise, the valleys of
      bliss, the veiny brooks
of deception, the early settlements of
      affection, the abandoned villages
of neglect, the star speckled deserts of
      honesty, the silent forests
of questions unasked, the irrigated fields of
      effort and hard work, the ridged mountains
of conflict, the ports of commitment, the

                        ocean of loss.
       When it was all done,
      I showed you the map, filled in
       with place names and street numbers,
   coffee shops, vegetable isles, park benches and airports;

                    complete with the milestones
                    of memory and aspiration;
                    peppered with
                    olive trees, almond blossoms,
                    rhododendrons, agave, roses and
                    walnut trees too.

You told me it looks pretty, it looks clear,   picked up your guitar
                                                  and sang of dawn
            and sleepless eyes   and how   no amount
of coordinates, delicately drawn
lines, contours, scales and grids
can ever tell   the truth   of the land.

Colonized

"Love affairs with people and places are sought out, lived and sometimes even end in the same way. We 'consume' them. They wear out. Taking it all in, becoming the other, is a transformation leading up to that assimilation. […] for amorous ingestion can be a way of devouring, another form of 'consumption.' Indeed the same emotional consumption affects both bodies and places."

— Giuliana Bruno, from *Atlas of Emotion*

The cord between
    us, worming its way through
        your navel, weaving
            past your bowels,
                celiac artery, to my heart —
                    boa constrictor.
                        I have seen a snake
                            swallow a deer after crushing
                      its lungs
                    its spindly calves
              marrow gushing, the fight
        smothered out —
ready for consumption.

Retina, cornea, iris
    laser beam whip
        invisible sting
            wraps around and
                tasers the heart –
                    writhing the helpless doe,
                        shattered the willowy body,
                    the membrane soul.

                Diphthong tongue
            flicking jugs of word glass
      holding half the
    venom, the other half
in the vapour and light
      of cobwebbed streetlamps,
        the tear gas language
            that envelopes, infiltrates,
                penetrates
                    intoxicates,
                assimilates
                    eradicates.

        It doesn't take much
           to chip
      the tessellated anatomy –
           a fractured

sentence,   a ruptured
word to   drive the
cleavage   deep
grooved   red.

You.

The power you

abuse, sly and achingly transparent

like a beating on

the sole.

Standing on the Sun

iii

You write home and hope
the letter will transcend the planes
you have thawed. Your body is free and
you are free
of your body. You no longer need
the train to haul it from here to
there — this shell of a
home you could not shed. Could it
shed you? Evict you
like a sigh. How strong is the mortar,
how solid is the door?
You no longer have
to remain within
the boundaries of flesh and skin
and blood and bone and all the matter in
between that translates the outside
for the inside
so you may move and nod and
understand and stand
up and defy
the status quo. You are the status
quo that no one knows
but no one can deny.

Στενάχωρο

For Mami

[Στεναχώρια – στενός (narrow) + χώρος (space) – unpleasant emotional state, discomfort, frustration, sadness, sorrow, grief, bitterness]

      All in one word
        you   told me
      how it   feels
     to put feet with
bunion   wings
   into a shoe that
       should
          fit.

Bimarian

To be the sea – to be the ocean;
        the sweet plucking of the
baglama, the rumbling currents of the
        cello – I trace my blood through
blue-green veinous rivers as they tangle in a cross-
        atlantic knot;
I hear them all – white manes combing
        through the wind.

Bitter to the tongues in
        my mouth, sharp against
my throat, my chords beat
        against the rocks, undulating
a web of coloured threads
        clashing, clashing,
crashing against the semantic
        fields I hold up like a referee.

To be the haphazardly
        constructed ball
of rubber bands, a bird's
        nest of mud and twigs and DNA,
the tangled delta of earphones
        at the bottom of a rucksack crooning
chanting, belting at least two
        different songs.

The sand knows what my feet
        deny; little piglets running all the way
home, the way home, the way
        home – can you tell
the beginning from the end of
        the isthmus, the strait, the offing;
what lies beyond? What lies beneath –
        wine dark mass my ampulla won't fit.

Native Stranger

I lie barefoot and shrimp eyed
in a city that sleeps with a gaping
mouth of ruins.

Here is where   the old man sings
here is where   catcalls ring
here is where   the smells
     of roasting meat and garlic pierce the air
here is where hours pass and coffee cools,
     concrete meets marble, old meets new
here is where day broke and we stumbled into
     the church and closed our eyes,
here is where we've said goodbye, too many times,
     to the sound of approaching trains.

'Round cityscapes of beer bottles
voices intersect   speaking a language I can
     understand, a language rooted
     in the land, tightly woven through my
     spine, a language I can use, a language
I can't curse in   a language
I don't dream in.

Home is where
no one expects the shoe to fit

where no one is surprised I need
a bigger size, a different
size, a different shoe
altogether.

I lie barefoot and shrimp eyed,
my gaping mouth of ruins
out of joint
with a city that cannot help
but be home.

Standing on the Sun

iv

You took the polar express,
or something like it,
somewhere
where - and here
is here and here and you don't have
to use the dictionary, or the rail
tracks of syntax. Language is no longer fact
or epexegesis. The black inscrutable lines no longer
bother you. You have no
fear that this mobile army of metaphors
will corner you. You have no fear that
it will evade you. You have
no fear, no need, for Ithacas are not
made of diamonds. Just
a seed you will toss
behind that you will not wait to hear
drop amidst the pebbles between
the tracks. Your compass is not
cracked or confused
pointing
north or south or west or east,
up or down or in or out,
pointing
right or wrong.

It is obsolete. There is no guarantee
you will find your way. But you will find
a way. Convoluted, serpentine, aquiline –
boundless
neutrino on the sun, you are not
obsolete, yet.

On a Winter Morning

Crisp air, muted, the
sky a swallow's petrol back,
eburnean belly

stalactites dicho-
tomize celestial swords –
phrenic refraction

your lilac sunrise
echoes against cardinal
rooftops the threshold

of my mind rever-
berates, splinter vacuum in
the stalactite, ice

on the butterfly
kissed petals – bloodshot eyeballs
silver chime dissolved

Time over Place over You over Me

There was a time when God
used to perch on windowsills
and green grapes, the
        Virgin Mary winked
        in the flickering lights
        of the carpeted bathroom and
            shadows cast at night
            in the windowless hallway
            formed angels out of hexagons.
There was a time   but is
    for the place that is   no more.

+

            If I could lasso the fireworks
            dispersing under the calvarium
            dome, harness the hushed
        tornado, catch the whistle
        before the heat rises through
        the nozzle on the brink
of sound, the brink of the big
bang – in the millisecond before
a sneeze

I would insert a doorstop of chipped
                 oak and felt tip pen
                 faces from a mahogany afternoon
                 when or
where bodies were   but are
                 in places that are   no more.

Gathering Crumbs

For Grandma Estela

She gathers the crumbs

on the kitchen table, handmade mosaic

a geologist's tender fancy – but

her thoughts hover over a time

before the time before –

hands with too much skin

streaked grey and blue-green canals;

seasoned gondolier.

Lake in Chapala ripples

with the weight of shoes, hooves,

sweet milk and pungent cheese

carried along the ceaseless friction of cicadas –

colourful skirts twirl and echo

the mariachis' sombreros, suitors miss

their kisses and leave with the sting

of an earring against their cheeks.

Times before the collision of life
against the living room carpet;
seven hungry mouths hanging from a string —
she doesn't speak of the dark ages.

But she gathers the crumbs on the kitchen table
even after there are no crumbs left
collecting every last piece,
taps the table and folds

those hands with too much skin
streaked grey and blue-green canals
into her lap — opens her eyes,
glazed but sharp enough to almost say:

keep these crumbs,
they're yours now.

Standing on the Sun

v

The sun a mandar
in your palm – fine lines – runes –
ashes snowball through

sea-bed air – the ink
the curlicues of tele
kinesis – and fact –

notes that dissipate –
a dancer's swan-necked wrists –
a physicist's per

haps an algebraic
symmetry in the amoeba
or you or you and

me that cannot help
but be – a construct – a dis
appearing act – a

magician you can
not see – a puppeteer you
aim to be – to be

*the limbs that hold the
strings — to weave them in and out
and through the space that*

*sculpts you with a god
ly indifference — take it back.
The sun a mandar*

in your palm.